The Fourth Wise Man

by Elizabeth Hale

Based on *The Story of the Other Wise Man*
by Henry Van Dyke.
(Published by Hodder and Stoughton)

NATIONAL CHRISTIAN EDUCATION COUNCIL
Robert Denholm House
Nutfield, Redhill, RH1 4HW

No performance of this play may be given without the written permission of the National Christian Education Council to whom all applications for performing rights should be made, enclosing a reply paid envelope.

Normally no performing rights fee will be charged for performances presented in a church or church hall for which there is no admission charge.

The performance time is approximately 20 minutes.

Published by:
National Christian Education Council
Robert Denholm House
Nutfield
Redhill RH1 4HW

British Library Cataloguing-In-Publication Data:
Hale, Elizabeth
   The fourth wise man
   I. Title
   822'.914

ISBN 0-7197-0571-1

First published 1988
© Elizabeth Hale

All rights reserved. No part of this play may be reproduced in any form or by any means without the prior permission in writing of the publisher.

Printed in Great Britain by Page Bros (Norwich) Ltd

The Fourth Wise Man

CAST
in order of appearance

ZANDA	a traveller
HELENA	a peasant woman
ARTABAN	an astrologer
ABGARUS	Father of Artaban
ZANDA	(as a child)
OLD MAN	
HANNAH	a Jewish woman
SOLDIER	

STAGING

As the story is told in a series of 'flash backs', a divided stage is needed. The Inner Stage should suggest a tree – shadowed space outside a small stone house with small stools for seats. The Outer Stage needs no scenery, but one or two stools are useful. Both stages need independent lighting, so that the lights can reveal the Inner or Outer Stage as the play suggests.

PROLOGUE

This takes place on the Inner Stage. A woman, perhaps between 25–30 years of age is sitting on a stool carding some sheep's wool. A traveller enters. He is 45 to 50 years old and his robes, though somewhat shabby, are colourfully embroidered and suggest that he comes from the East. He wears, hanging from a chord round his neck, a gold medallion engraved with a pair of wings. He approaches the woman and puts down the pack which he has been carrying on his shoulder. He wipes his forehead.

ZANDA   The sun is high and I should like to rest. Will you permit me to enjoy the shade of your trees for a while?

HELENA   Gladly. I will bring a stool and some wine. You look hot and weary.

She goes off stage, returning with a stool. She offers him a cup of wine which he drinks thirstily. He hands back the cup with a little bow, before sitting.

ZANDA   A cup of wine was never more welcome, nor tasted more delicious. My compliments to you, lady.

HELENA *(looking pleased. Sits)* My wine is known around here for its flavour. It's a good place for grapes and all kinds of fruits. We do well.

ZANDA *(pointing to the wool which she has taken up again)* I see you are preparing some wool. It is from your own sheep?

HELENA   Yes, our flocks prosper and my husband is a careful shepherd who finds the best grazing for the animals.

There is a pause as ZANDA looks around him. He sighs.

ZANDA   How peaceful it is here. This place makes me regret my decision to journey once again to Jerusalem. *(Smiling ruefully)* I must be getting old.

HELENA *(with interest)* You are going to Jerusalem? *(He nods).* But, you are not a Jew.

ZANDA   No, my home is far away in the East, but I visited Jerusalem many times with an old friend who is now, unhappily, dead. So this is by way of being a pilgrimage.

HELENA   A pilgrimage? Will you visit the place where he died to pay your respects?

ZANDA   I should like to do that, but it will be difficult. I was not with him on that occasion and now several years have passed and it will be hard to find anyone who remembers.

HELENA *(curiously)* This friend of your's; was he a merchant?

ZANDA *(smiling)* No, not a merchant. *(Very proudly)* He was an astrologer!

HELENA *(impressed)* An astrologer? One who studies the stars and can tell the future?

ZANDA   He was a man of great learning and much wisdom. I believe there were but three others like him in all our land.

HELENA   But why should an eastern astrologer go to Jerusalem? I do not think the Jews encourage such fore-telling. They live by the law.

ZANDA   That is true: but it is a very long story.

HELENA *(drawing her stool closer)* Will you tell it to me? *(Pause)* We are very quiet here, and when the traders rest by our house I love to hear them talk of other people and far-away places. Please – I should be so interested.

ZANDA *(pausing briefly)* Then I shall tell you the story of Artaban, the Magus. It is a story I have told to no one else, but something in my heart tells me it is not just curiosity which prompts your interest. I should like to share it with you. *(Long pause)*
My name is Zanda. It all began when, as a child, I

was a servant in the house of Abgarus, father of Artaban.

Lights fade on Inner Stage and go up on Outer Stage.

SCENE 1

The lights come up on the Outer Stage to reveal ARTABAN, a tall, strong man of about 40, with the eyes of a dreamer, but a resolute mouth. He is dressed in a long, white robe over a coloured tunic and wears a white pointed hat. Around his neck hangs a gold medallion on which is engraved a pair of wings. He stands looking out, as if into the heavens.

As he stands, his father ABGARUS enters. He is old, but still upright, and dignified. He wears a brightly coloured robe with a gold collar, the sign of a noble.

ABGARUS *(looking round, surprised at finding his son alone)* I heard the sound of horses. Have your brother astrologers no time to share your studies tonight?

ARTABAN *(coming towards him)* It seems not, father. I *know* the time is right for us to undertake a journey, but each of my colleagues has more pressing demands to satisfy; the care of the royal treasure; the claims of a new bride; the limitations imposed by ill-health.

ABGARUS *(fondly)* And I, my son, am too old to go wherever your quest leads you, but I should like to know your plans.

He sits attentively.

ARTABAN *(taking two small linen scrolls which have been tucked inside his girdle)* Look at these, father. *(He sits near him, and unrolls one scroll)* Here is a prophecy of the Jews, that from them shall come a Saviour into the world.

ABGARUS *(interrupting sharply)* Since when does the noble Persian Magus read of Jewish prophecies? For centuries the Jews have been a conquered race: conquered by Assyrians, Babylonians, and our great King Cyrus. They are scattered among every nation, and the poor

	remnant which remains in Judea is subject to Rome. You cannot believe these writings to have any significance?
ARTABAN	Please, let me finish, father. Here is the second scroll, from the time of Cyrus. Here we have times and dates for the coming of the Anointed One.
ABGARUS	And you have made calculations?
ARTABAN	Yes. I and three fellow Magi, Caspar, Melchior, and Balthazar, have searched the ancient writings and have drawn conclusions. In the spring we saw in the heavens, Jupiter and Saturn drawing together in the sign of the Fish, which is the sign of the House of the Hebrews, and there was a new star which shone for one night only. *(He rises and looks out)* Tonight those two planets will meet again and we four are watching. If we see the new star again, we have agreed to set out and meet together within ten days at the ancient Temple in Babylon. If it continues to shine we shall set out for Jerusalem, to find the new-born King of Israel.
ABGARUS	*(rising and putting his hand on his son's shoulder)* I fear you will be disappointed, my son, but you must pursue your calling. Have you sufficient means to sustain your journey?
ARTABAN	Yes, I have sold my house and possessions and I have bought these.

> *He takes out of his girdle a small leather bag and pours its contents into his hand.*

A sapphire, a ruby, and a pearl. I shall carry them with me as a tribute to the King *(Pause)* I wish you could come with me.

ABGARUS *(moving away)* I shall be with you in spirit, my son, and I can at least lend you Zanda to be your companion and helper. I will send him to you. Go in peace.

> *Exit.*
>
> *ARTABAN returns to his star-gazing and is so*

intent he doesn't notice the entrance of ZANDA, a young boy about 10 years old.

ZANDA   Master Artaban . . .

ARTABAN   Hush, Zanda. This is a very special moment. Look carefully, there, where my finger points. What do you see?

ZANDA   Stars, Master.

ARTABAN   Yes, stars, of course, but there, do you not see the great planets and that bright new star that winks and shines beside them?

ZANDA   Yes, I see it *(Pause)* I think.

ARTABAN   But we are wasting time. Saddle my horse, Zanda, and let us be on our way.

Both exit.

Lights come up on the Inner Stage.

ZANDA   We rode for days, Master Artaban and I. Oh, it was exciting for me, child that I was, to sit up in front of the great Magus, encircled by his noble arms. I shall never forget all we saw; the high mountains; the rushing rivers; the wild horses thundering across the plains and birds crying in the swamps. By nightfall on the tenth day we had reached the approaches to Babylon and had until midnight to find its famous Temple. A direct route lay through a grove of date-palms, and there occurred a strange thing. Our horse, after first slowing, then hesitating, at last refused to enter. As we came to a halt, a low moaning sound made my master dismount and go forward on foot.

Lights fade on ZANDA and come up on the Outer Stage to show ARTABAN cautiously approaching the figure of a man, lying face down, on the ground. ZANDA follows at a safe distance.

ARTABAN   *(crouching over the man)* I was sure I heard moaning, but it seems to me that he is dead.

He picks up the man's hand, then lets it go lifelessly to the ground.

ZANDA *(approaching cautiously)* Is he a Babylonian?

ARTABAN   I don't think so. His robe suggests that he is a Jew; perhaps a descendant of one of the exiles who never returned to Judea when Cyrus gave them their freedom. His skin looks dry and yellow, as if he has had a fever. There is nothing we can do for him.

> *He rises and as he turns to move away, the hand of the man on the ground moves to fasten on the hem of ARTABAN'S robe, and a slight moan escapes his lips. ARTABAN pauses.*

ZANDA *(pulling his hand)* Come, Master, we shall be late at the temple.

ARTABAN *(looking down at the man)* He is *not* dead, Zanda. How can we leave him?

ZANDA *(pulling his hand more urgently)* We must, Master. The Magi will leave without us. Perhaps this man's friends have gone for help and will be back soon.

ARTABAN   Yes, that must be so. Surely he would not be left to die alone.

> *He tries to move away, but the hand still grips his robe and another moan is heard.*

How firmly he grips me. I cannot abandon him now, Zanda. Go to the horse and bring the water bottle here.

ZANDA   But, Master, we shall be late.

ARTABAN   Do as I say, Zanda. We may yet restore him.

> *ZANDA exits and ARTABAN raises the old man and pulls him across the ground, to prop him against a tree. When ZANDA returns he gives him a drink and also wipes his face with a cloth. He speaks to the old Jew in a gentle voice.*

Here take some water first, then I will mix a potion from my special herbs. It will do you good.

> *He takes a small packet from his girdle, empties the contents into a cup of water and makes the*

old man drink. ZANDA watches impatiently. After a time the old man seems to regain vigour.

OLD MAN *(in a faint voice)* Who are you?, and why have you come to restore me to life?

ARTABAN I am Artaban, the Magus, from the city of Ecbatana in Persia, and I'm on my way to Jerusalem to search for the great Deliverer, the one who is to be born, King of the Jews. *(Rising)* I must not stay any longer with you or my friends will go without me, but I will leave you bread and wine, *(He motions ZANDA who fetches a bundle which he puts on the ground near the old man)* and more of my healing herbs.

OLD MAN *(raising a trembling hand)* May the God of Abraham, Isaac and Jacob bless you on your journey. I have nothing with which I can repay you for your kindness to me, except to tell you where you will find the Messiah. He will not be born in Jerusalem, but in Bethlehem, David's town. May the Lord guide you in safety because you had pity on me.

Lights fade on Outer Stage as ZANDA and ARTABAN go off.

Lights come up on ZANDA and HELENA again on Inner Stage.

ZANDA It was already past midnight and we made as much haste as we could to reach the Temple before the three Magi set off, but it was dawn before we got there and there was no one to be seen. Artaban was *so* discouraged. Up and down the terraces he walked, scanning the distant horizons.

Lights fade on Inner Stage and rise on the Outer Stage to show ARTABAN and ZANDA searching around. Suddenly ZANDA lets out a cry.

ZANDA Master! Master!

ARTABAN What is it? What have you found?

ZANDA Here, Master, near these stones. There's a piece of parchment. Is it a letter for you?

ARTABAN *(picking up the parchment and reading it)* Yes, just as I thought. They could not wait beyond midnight, so have gone ahead. They ask me to follow them across the desert. *(He sits down with his head in his hands)* How can I cross the desert? We have no food, and the horse is exhausted.

ZANDA *(encouragingly)* We could go into Babylon for provisions, Master, and perhaps we could buy a camel for the journey.

ARTABAN You are right not to be discouraged, Zanda. Yes, we *must* go on. I shall have to sell my sapphire to pay for what we need, but I still have two gifts for the King. Surely God will not deny me the sight of the Messiah because I was delayed by an act of mercy.

> *Lights fade on Outer Stage as ZANDA and ARTABAN go off. Lights rise on the Inner Stage to show ZANDA and HELENA.*

ZANDA In Babylon my Master sold his sapphire and bought provisions and a camel for our journey. What a very uncomfortable animal the camel is. It is rightly called 'the ship of the desert', for truly it pitches and rocks its passengers much like a ship in a storm. *(HELENA laughs at the thought)* I cannot say that I enjoyed that part of the journey, and the desert was a frightening place. I shall never forget the skull-like rocks, the dried-up river beds and the never-ending sand dunes. By day the intense heat kept all the lizards asleep, out of sight, and at night, as the star continued to shine above us, the cold kept us awake, listening to the prowling jackals. *(HELENA shivers)* Then, at last we reached Damascus, its gardens watered by ancient streams and growing roses more beautiful than any we had seen before. On we journeyed to Lake Galilee, the highlands of Judea, and finally, Bethlehem.

> *Lights fade on Inner Stage and rise again on the Outer Stage to show ARTABAN examining one of his scrolls.*

SCENE 2

ARTABAN *(calling ZANDA to him)* Look, Zanda, here is the writing which describes the Saviour, and this is the place of which the old Jew in Babylon told us.

ZANDA *(looking around)* But it's a very poor place, Master. Surely a great Prince would not be born in such a place as this. The old man must have been mistaken.

ARTABAN *(looking into his pouch containing the two remaining jewels)* I cannot believe that. Although the other Magi do not appear to be here, we have come swiftly and cannot be far behind them. Every night the star has shone above, us, leading us on, and now we shall surely find him and I have my gifts to offer.

ZANDA *(moving about the stage)* There is no-one about, Master. Where shall we enquire? I do not see any men here.

ARTEBAN Perhaps the men have gone to the pastures to bring down the sheep, but there is a cottage. No doubt the lady of the house will be able to help us.

As they approached the door, a woman's voice can be heard singing a lullaby. ARTABAN calls through the door-way.

Good day to you, lady. Could you help a stranger?

The lady of the house comes on stage, her baby in her arms, and looks curiously at the visitors.

HANNAH Peace be with you. *(Pause)* How can I help you? *(Pause)* Did I not see you in the village with the other nobles, three days ago?

ARTABAN No, lady, but you rejoice my heart when you speak of other travellers, for now I know truly that I have come to the right place. Where did they go?

HANNAH They went to the lodging house where a visitor from Nazareth, a man named Joseph, was staying with his wife, newly delivered of a son.

> *She looks fondly at her own baby.*

ARTABAN *(smilingly he repeats her words and looks triumphantly at ZANDA who is sitting on the ground taking a rest)* Delivered of a son!

HANNAH Yes, – what a night that was. Having so recently had a child myself the Inn-Keeper's wife asked if I would go to comfort and help the young mother. I was glad to do so, she was so young and it was her first baby.

> *Warming to her subject she sits down and indicates to ARTABAN that he should do the same.*

She was so calm, not a word of complaint at having had to make so long a journey in her condition, nor at having to give birth in such surroundings. I felt ashamed that we could do no better for them, but, with the census, all our houses were full, and we did what we could. The birth of every child is wonderful, but this one was particularly so.

ARTABAN *(leaning forward eagerly)* Why was that?

HANNAH Because everywhere was full of light. I can't explain it and have no words to say more. Everywhere was full of light.

ARTABAN Did you see the star?

HANNAH We all did, and when the astrologers came, they said it had led them to Bethelehem.

ARTABAN Did they visit the child?

HANNAH Yes. I'm told they worshipped him, and gave him rich gifts but I know no more.

ARTABAN How long did they stay?

HANNAH That's the strange part. They didn't stay but disappeared as suddenly as they had come. This alarmed the villagers; they had a feeling that something was wrong.

ARTABAN How strange, but I suppose they had accomplished their mission and had no cause to stay.

HANNAH That's true, but that same night, Joseph of Nazareth took his wife and son and fled, some said to Egypt.

Since then we have all been uneasy, almost as if a spell had been cast on the village by the evil one. Some say the Roman soldiers are coming to force more money from us in taxes, so our men-folk have taken our flocks and herds into the hills to avoid losing them. They are our wealth, without them we have nothing.

ARTABAN *(rising)* Thank you for talking to me. It seems that now I must follow the young family to Egypt.

HANNAH *(rising also)* Before you go, you must have some refreshment. It is a peasant fare, but wholesome, and, if you have water-bottles I will fill them for you.

She goes into the house.

ARTABAN *(shaking Zanda)* Wake up, Zanda, it is time to prepare to move on. Fetch the water-bottles to fill for our journey.

ZANDA *(rising reluctantly)* But, Master, isn't this Bethelehem?

ARTABAN Yes, it is, but my fellow astrologers were here three days ago and the new King has been taken to Egypt.

ZANDA Egypt! Master. Is it far?

ARTABAN Yes, very far. Fetch the water-bottles.

ZANDA Yes, Master. *(Grumbling as he goes out)* Not more camel rides!

HANNAH *(she has left the baby indoors and brings a dish of bread and fruit)* Will you sit and eat? *(ARTABAN does so)* The baby is asleep and I have time to minister to your needs.

ARTABAN You are very kind. *(He takes some food, but, suddenly, ZANDA rushes in, obviously frightened)*

ZANDA Master! Master!

ARTABAN *(rising)* What is it, Zanda? What has alarmed you?

ZANDA Soldiers, Master, with swords and spears!

HANNAH Soldiers? They have come sooner than we thought.

ARTABAN *(picking up the dish of food and giving it to her)* Go into the house and shut the door. Zanda, go with her. Do not wake the baby, and make no sound.

They go inside and ARTABAN stands in the doorway, filling the space with his height and broad shoulders.
One of Herod's SOLDIERS enters, with a drawn sword.

SOLDIER   Stand aside! We have orders from Herod to search every house.

ARTABAN   *(calmly)* For what purpose?

SOLDIER   Our orders are to kill all the male children, two years old and under. Rumours of the birth of a new born King have reached Herod. He will tolerate no rival. Stand aside.

ARTABAN   *(standing his ground)* I can assure you there is no need to search my house. I live alone.

SOLDIER   I have my orders. Stand aside.

ARTABAN   *(not moving but taking the pouch out of his belt)* I am all alone and wish to remain so. *(He pours a jewel into his hand and holds it out)* I am willing to give this ruby to any soldier who will forget his orders and leave me in peace.

SOLDIER   *(taking the stone, greedily)* What a beauty! I'm made for life. *(Loudly)* I'm sure I can take your word for it, sir. There's not likely to be a child in your house. I'll be on my way. *(He goes off, examining the stone)* What a beauty! This really *is* my lucky day!

ARTABAN   *(looking after him)* May God forgive me for my untruth, now two of my gifts have gone. I have given to men, those things that were meant for God. Shall I ever deserve to find the Saviour?

ZANDA reappears, followed by HANNAH who goes to ARTABAN and takes his hand.

HANNAH   You saved my son's life. I can find no other words, but to thank you. Every day of my life I shall pray that the Lord will bless you and give you his peace.

Lights fade on Outer Stage and rise again on the Inner Stage to show ZANDA and HELENA sitting as at the beginning.

SCENE 3

HELENA What a moving story. Your Master was indeed a wonderful man. Did he find the Saviour in Egypt?

ZANDA *(moving forward onto the Outer Stage)* No, after we left Nazareth, we journeyed to Egypt to try to find the young child with his parents, but no-where could we find any trace of such a family. I begged my Master to give up the search, which seemed to have become an obsession, but he would not hear of it. After the death of Herod, we returned to Judea, to Jerusalem always searching, searching, growing ever poorer and more dispirited. After many years, I felt we must part and I returned home, to the house of Abgarus, but the old man was dead, so I had to start to make a living for myself.

HELENA *(coming to join him)* But you never forgot Artaban?

ZANDA Never. When travellers returned from Judea I always asked around to see if anyone had news of him but none was sure where he was to be found. Then, about five years ago, I met up with some traders newly returned from Jerusalem and amongst their wares offered for sale I found this *(He takes off the medallion round his neck and holds it in his hand. He shows it to HELANA)* I knew it at once. See the mark on the back. It had belonged to Artaban. I bought it and questioned how they had come by it, but all they could tell me was that its owner had died in some kind of accident in the city. It comforts me to have it, but how I wish I knew what had happened and if Artaban ever found the Messiah.

HELENA May I see the medallion again? *(ZANDA hands it to her)* Yes, I thought so. It is the same.

ZANDA The same?

HELENA Yes, when you first greeted me, I noticed the pendant around your neck and I knew I had seen one like it somewhere before. Now I know where I saw it. *(Pause)* Your Master, Artaban, died saving my life.

ZANDA *(in amazement)* He saved your life? But this is amazing. Please tell me what happened. *(Both sit)*

HELENA My name is Helena and I am Greek. . . . My father was a merchant, not a very successful one, I'm afraid, and when he died he left me many debts. We were living just outside Jerusalem at the time, and those to whom my father owed money came to our house and took all we had of value. Everything was not enough, however, and, despite my mother's pleas for mercy, they seized me, saying I must be sold as a slave to repay what remained. *(She rises and walks forward as she remembers her story)*

They threw me across the saddle of a horse to take me into Jerusalem but when we reached the Damascus gate of the city we were met by a great crowd, all surging outwards, and shouting and pushing so that the horses could not enter. My captors dismounted and pulled me behind them as they tried to battle against the throng. In the crowd I saw a chance to escape and tried shouting for help, but no one was interested in a shabby slave girl. They were all going to see the execution outside the city walls at Golgotha; two thieves and a prophet called Jesus of Nazareth.

ZANDA *(interrupting)* Did you say Jesus . . . of Nazareth? Oh, surely they would not have killed a prophet!

HELENA Not the people, they loved him as one sent by God to do wonderful works, but the priests and elders were jealous and had forced Pilate to condemn him because they said he had claimed to be the King of the Jews.

ZANDA The King of the Jews! Then if you met Artaban in Jerusalem he must have found the King.

HELENA *(sitting)* Again, he came too late. Suddenly, I caught sight of him in the crowd, his robes old and shabby, but unmistakeably the robes of a Magus, and he was wearing the medallion you showed me. He seemed my only hope of escape, so I wrenched myself from my captors and fell at his feet imploring his help. Although old, he still had strength in his arms as he drew me to my feet and placed me behind him as he faced my pursuers. He put his hand to his belt and drew out a little pouch and from it he took the most beautiful pearl. This he placed in my hand. He told me he had thought to use it to buy freedom for Jesus – a kind of ransome to save his life – but instead he gave it to me to keep me from slavery. *(She is overcome as she remembers)*

ZANDA *(emotionally)* Oh, Master! Master!

HELENA *(now recovered)* When my tormentors had gone, pleased with their prize, I stayed with the old man, struggling and failing to find words to express my gratitude. Suddenly everything became dark, although it was the middle of the day, and the earth shook. We crouched by a house wall and your Master protected me with his body as stones crashed down. I was terrified and cried aloud in fear as yet another tremor shook the wall's foundations. Tiles, shaken from the roofs, fell everywhere, and your master gasped and collapsed on top of me. I knew he had been hit. I crawled out and bent over him. There was a wound in his temple, and I thought he was dead. I wept as I cradled his head in my arms, and then his lips moved. I had to bend closer to hear what he said and today I still remember every word.

ZANDA *(quietly)* Please tell me. It will comfort me.

HELENA *(rising)* These were his words. 'Lord when did I see you hungry and fed you, or thirsty and gave you a drink? When did I see you a stranger and took you in, or naked and clothed you? When did I see you sick or in prison and came to you? I have looked for you for 33 years and I have never seen your face nor ministered to you, my King.'

Then, I seemed to hear another voice from far away, which said, 'As you have done it to the least of these

	my brothers, you have done it to me.' *(She pauses)* A wonderful smile lit your Master's face and he died. *(There is a long pause, and HELENA sits)*
ZANDA	Thank you. Now I too can be at peace with myself. *(He rises)* Please keep the medallion. Artaban's journey has ended, his treasures have been offered and accepted. *(Pause)* I know now that the fourth wise man found his King. *(Lights fade)*

CURTAIN

Drama Resources from NCEC

Zealot

Christine Wass

A refreshingly new Easter play for production by young people and/or adults.

ISBN 0-7197-0513-4

Putting on a Performance

A practical guide covering all aspects of producing musicals and plays

ISBN 0-7197-0560-6

Send for complete list to NCEC, Robert Denholm House, Nutfield, Redhill RH1 4HW